Ma   f
BY Duffers

CW00867740

With best wishes to
Anna

[signature]

[signature]
Best wishes to you
15-2-2017

Management By Duffers

B. BALASUBRAMANIAM

Cartoons by Ms. Gayathri

Notion Press

Old No. 38, New No. 6
McNichols Road, Chetpet
Chennai - 600 031

First Published by Notion Press 2017
Copyright © B. Balasubramaniam 2017
All Rights Reserved.

ISBN 978-1-946641-95-3

This book has been published with all reasonable efforts taken to make the material error-free after the consent of the author. No part of this book shall be used, reproduced in any manner whatsoever without written permission from the author, except in the case of brief quotations embodied in critical articles and reviews.

The Author of this book is solely responsible and liable for its content including but not limited to the views, representations, descriptions, statements, information, opinions and references ["Content"]. The Content of this book shall not constitute or be construed or deemed to reflect the opinion or expression of the Publisher or Editor. Neither the Publisher nor Editor endorse or approve the Content of this book or guarantee the reliability, accuracy or completeness of the Content published herein and do not make any representations or warranties of any kind, express or implied, including but not limited to the implied warranties of merchantability, fitness for a particular purpose. The Publisher and Editor shall not be liable whatsoever for any errors, omissions, whether such errors or omissions result from negligence, accident, or any other cause or claims for loss or damages of any kind, including without limitation, indirect or consequential loss or damage arising out of use, inability to use, or about the reliability, accuracy or sufficiency of the information contained in this book.

Dedicated to My Parents

CONTENTS

Preface of Book

Management is defined as the art of skilful administering of a group of persons and material resources to achieve a desired goal. At the centre of this skilful administering is the contriver who holds the reins and controls the activities of all members of his team - this person is looked upon by his subordinates as 'The Manager' or 'The Boss'.

Skilful administration comes from:

1. Knowledge - that can be acquired.
2. Assertiveness to vindicate one's action - that is innate in one's nature and is proportional to acquired knowledge and
3. An upright character - which manifests as one's reputation.

It has to be realised that one who aspires for growth in one's career has to necessarily pass through the portals of:

1. Qualification (either formal or informal) - that is based on one's aptitude.
2. Education - that one acquires while honing one's aptitude by 'hands on training' and which leans heavily on one's attitude.

3. Knowledge - that inspires confidence amongst colleagues and is the first milestone one has to reach to be considered a 'trouble shooter' and

4. Wisdom - the aura of invincibility that others see around you.

However, it is regrettable that many a person rarely crosses the first two portals in his entire career.

In the first two phases of Qualification and Education, monetary benefit is one of the prime motivating factors and in the next two phases of Knowledge and Wisdom, it's pride that drives the individual and it's only at this stage that one becomes 'The Boss'.

With the proliferation of institutions that profess to churn out instant 'Bosses', skill has become the first casualty and has been replaced by guile. It's this guile that is being substituted for knowledge that provides for many a comical interlude in the process of attempting 'Skilful Administration'.

This book of quips is based on incidents that are almost a daily occurrence in establishments and organisations that arise in the 'Boss–Subordinate' relationship.

The cartoons by my wife, Gayathri, have enhanced the book a myriad times.

I wish to express my gratitude to the authors whose quotes have been used to derive some of the quips to highlight an act of Management.

I trust that this book will be a welcome read to all persons who are managing something in their lives and I am sure they will identify with some of the quips and cartoons as being their 'work in progress' and leave a smile on their faces.

MANAGEMENT QUIPS

What all Executives should know

If your idea of pleasing your boss means having to say 'Yes, Sir'! 'Yes, Sir'! all the time, then the chances of getting three bags of wool as salary should not be ruled out.

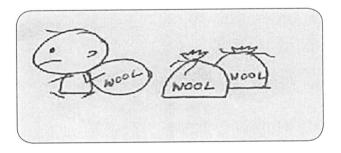

Remember a feather in your cap does not entitle you to fly.

Its fine when you are your boss' pet. However, it's only when you submit your medical bills for reimbursement that you will notice that they will be returned as not having come from your authorised doctor - the Vet.

Do not be carried away by the pep talk of seniors when they tell you solutions to problems are always guided by: "Where there is a will there is a way"; when in reality it is: "Where is the way to the will?"

If your subordinate poses a problem that is way beyond your comprehension, do not get pegged down by your ignorance; just pretend to contemplate - the 'solution' to the problem may be just two 'pegs' away.

Always attribute delays in meeting deadlines to a bug in the software you were working on - it enhances your reputation, even if you were the bug.

Remember your chances of success in the organisation are directly proportional to your ability to camouflage your ignorance, deride your peers and terrorise your subordinates - all your bosses see themselves in you.

Try being a recluse; it makes you look like a genius even if you are a dud.

If you want to be the boss – fine - but do not make your subordinates feel you are a 'Boss stud'.

It is better to rise on the palms of your subordinates than on the boots of your superiors.

An employee who is not a team man and always thinks he is 'the benchmark of perfection', is not aware that in the opinion of his peers and subordinates he is 'the perfect one to be on the bench'.

You will be appreciated not because you did your job well but because you did your boss' job well.

Remember, the person who nods the most at the meeting is just trying to fight sleep.

Corollary

The sacrificial lamb nods the most

Always delegate your failures and cling onto others' successes.

Remember management never practices what the Bible preaches-it permits the boss to cast a stone even if he is a sinner.

For those managing projects - when an upstart reaches the top, 'startup' slides down.

Remember heaven and hell are akin to an organisation – all workers land up in heaven and lead an idle life with no one to instruct them as all the managers are in hell bellowing instructions on how they should be saved from the frying pans even while there are none to heed them. This is why heaven is id(y)l (e)lic and peaceful.

Remember, in any Management meeting there will be two Managers with divergent ideas, forcefully remonstrating that their idea will converge at the desired goal, while the rest of the managers like 'statistics' will support both the sides leading to a stalemate. This will lead to series of meetings, till at one stage the goal disappears.

Remember that no one ever died defending a cause, he died not knowing how to defend himself.

Remember that when the going gets tough the tough get going home - it's the meek that stay till the end and get the blame.

Remember that punishment is inversely proportional to the level in the hierarchy.

Remember the rules in life and in work are diametrically opposite —in life you will be condoned for all the wrong judgments made in your youth while at work you can only make a wrong judgment when you have the experience and the rank.

Remember weather predictions in a meteorology station are made most of the time by asking the gardener his opinion on the day's weather– it may be worthwhile getting the opinion of the janitor on all corporate matters, he may have sweeping solutions to your problems.

Remember your work place is a menagerie – initially you slog like a dog - barking, biting and wagging your tail, till you reach a level in the Management when you purr like a cat and think of only comfort and finally you become a scapegoat.

Remember when you feel strongly about an issue and put your foot down strongly don't put it on your other foot and become handicapped.

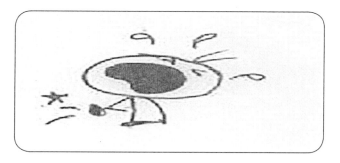

If you want to be the boss' pet you may have to work from his kennel.

Bosses never tire of 'blowing their own dumb pets'

Remember your success depends on identifying your colleagues: when a problem arises, the knowledgeable analyse the problem, the pretender circumvents the problem and the vast majority who are ignorant have to be kept off the problem.

Corollary

The knowledgeable are confident, the pretenders noisy and the ignorant are at meetings discussing the problem.

Remember taking part in a discussion on a subject that you are ignorant about is like the saying about the zipper on your fly – "opened when not necessary can embarrass you and closed when necessary can still embarrass you".

Early in your career know your capability – remember the enemy of the mud pot is the brass pot – if you are a 'mutt' pot be with the other 'mutt' pots avoid the "top brass" pots.

Remember that 'united you are a herd and divided you are a nerd'.

Corollary

A nerd is one who strays from the herd and becomes dinner.

An ignorant person is rarely brash unless he is the boss-remember the saying 'timidity is a protection from ignorance'.

Corollary

A suspicious nature is the by product of one's ignorance

Remember, when your query is answered quickly and wrongly that you have addressed your boss.

Remember the only 'solution ' you get at meetings is 'tea' but the consolation is that during the period of the meeting the originators of the problems being discussed are confined to the persons around the meeting table! Hence, no new problems are likely to crop up during the tenure of the meeting.

Remember the reasons for failures need not be looked for beyond the members of the meeting. However, the blame for the failure will surely be someone beyond the members of the meeting.

Remember when the CEO makes a flaw it is an aberration, when the executive makes a flaw it is oversight , when a supervisor makes a flaw it is an error and when a workman makes a flaw it is sabotage.

Remember the terms proprietary, state of the art machinery, fully automated, highly skilled work force are used by companies that are on the verge of bankruptcy, looking to change hands.

Remember success comes to people who never reach their goals also - like Columbus who tried to reach Malabar in the spice coast of South India but by a vast margin of error ended up in the Americas and yet became a celebrity.

Remember, sometimes not doing anything also gets you accolades - during the time you were idle the problem you were supposed to attend to got rectified while your colleague was attending to some other problem-this is known as 'collateral rectification'.

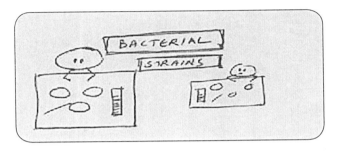

Remember a decision is always made from a set of alternatives – if you do not make the decision, you become one of the alternatives.

Remember no one uses reverse engineering like the Management - if you cannot 'overturn' problems then you become the 'turnover'.

Remember it's only the boss who can be called patient or a strategist when he seeks more time for solving the problem – for which he has no clue on the solution - others are dubbed inefficient.

Remember qualification and education are what an individual may possess but its only knowledge and wisdom that others will get to see in the individual if he ever possesses it.

When your boss tells you that problems, like animals, should be confronted headlong and you are encouraged to go for the jugular - make sure that the problem does not come in the form of a giraffe.

Workers and Management are like a nut and bolt - united they hold the company, divided they rust and end up in the scrap yard.

Corollary

Workers and Management are like a Nut and Bolt - Given work, workers 'bolt' and managers go 'nuts'

When the overworked 'mover and shaker' beats his chest it's not elation; it's a heart attack.

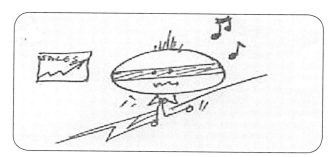

A person brags because he is sure no one believes him.

Most of the time your education helps you to tell your bosses what the problem actually is but it is your workers' wisdom that solves the problem. Hence always remember that the person who expresses the problem is always in management and the person who solves the problem is always a worker.

Remember that a University degree is just the doorway to education - like hunger is to enjoying food.

Qualification should be the funnel that allows you to enter the portals of education, knowledge and wisdom and not a bubble that encapsulates you and prevents you from becoming educated, knowledgable and wise

Corollary

Most senior qualified officials live in their own bubble —thinking they are well qualified for their job —only to realise that in a few years' time they have become like the bubbles in a paper weight.

A Manager who does not know an iota of the nature of the problem and how it occurred, continuously keeps berating his subordinates for lack of knowledge - with a fond hope that they will explain in 'layman' terms the nature of the problem and the possible solutions, so that he can explain the same to his bosses - preferably with a PowerPoint presentation - and be considered a top notch 'Troubleshooter' even while his subordinates realise that he is the 'Trouble' while they are 'Shooting' the problem.

Remember how Faraday kicked the apparatus he was experimenting on in disgust at not getting the desired result and noticed the galvanometer flicker – that brought about the famous law of electromagnetic induction –try the same when you are frustrated by not finding solutions; especially if you are in maintenance, it works at times.

If you wriggle and bend a lot all the time to please your boss, you may end up as a worm in a fishing hook.

Hierarchy in an Organisation is always divided into three groups - Executives, Supervisors and Workers. They are akin to an electric bulb; the filament is the worker, the glass the executive and the screw cap the supervisor. The going being good is akin to the filament glowing, the glass radiating the light and the supervisor staying firmly screwed. When the going is tough, the filament fuses, the glass does not radiate any light but it's the supervisor who stays firmly screwed.

Corollary

Supervisors are like jam between two slices of bread —one being the executive and the other the worker. It's the supervisor who can be 'licked' all the time.

Remember highly skilled craftsmen are always workers while highly unskilled crafty men are always in Management.

Hierarchy in an establishment is like a brick wall; the top layers are the easiest to remove.

Hierarchy amongst Management is akin to mobile phones – the lower ones have SIM cards with minimum talk time while bosses have FIM (Foot in the Mouth) cards with unlimited talk time.

Remember that the Julius Caesar of the corporate world – The CEO - always exits by saying 'Et Tu Brute' to the members of the board. The incoming CEO always starts by being Mark Anthony and gives his maiden speech praising the last CEO and then dons the mantle of Julius Caesar - waiting his turn.

Sycophancy is an art where you can bask in the warmth of your present boss and get scorched in the fury of your next boss.

Mentoring is the art of explaining to your subordinate that your company is the finest because of your efforts even while you have not got the due recognition.

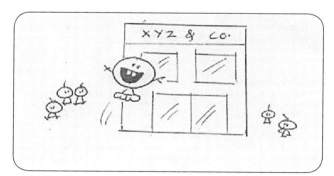

An inefficient employee always piggy backs on a good employee-but leapfrogs at an opportune moment to a higher level - overtaking the good employee, that is why higher levels are filled with shady 'toadies' who tend to 'croak' under their burden of responsibilities.

When a failure occurs, everyone says the systems are in 'place' to take care of any eventuality - but unfortunately the 'place' got misplaced in this instance.

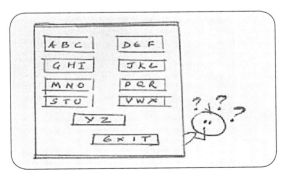

If you want to be applauded for your work
- remember the saying-"it's the applause
that killed the mosquito".

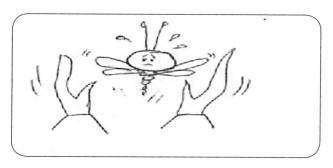

The junior whom the boss turns to
for a solution is invariably the most
hardworking - the early to bed and the
early to rise type - who will acquire
neither health nor wealth nor vice.

Get into the shoes of your subordinate to actually see the problem being faced only if the shoes are expensive and you can walk away with them.

When you always hog the limelight- you will be treated like a hog by your colleagues.

Code for meetings (1) Meetings are always held to unanimously accept the proposals put forward by the Chairman even if they are not feasible and (2) The Chairman holds the inalienable right to blame whomsoever he wishes for the failure in implementation of his proposals (3) the Chairman like the king in the story who even while being naked was praised for his fine clothes, should always be praised for his ideas even when you feel they are 'stupid'. (4) anyone intending to dissent should be a newcomer to the meeting and while the committee appreciates his views, they also regret that such a brilliant person has to leave the services of the company for personal reasons and wishes him well in all his future endeavors.

Remember that while knowledge can make one arrogant, wisdom makes one humble.

Corollary

Cockiness does not reflect knowledge; or being too reserved, wisdom

Help and helpless are what define the relationship between subordinate and boss - when you want help your boss is always helpless.

The line that divides the oppressor and the orphan is the same that divides Management and Workers.

Management is a haystack and a good manager a needle.

Corollary

When there is a burning problem most of the managers get reduced to ashes; only, the managers of steel get better tempered.

Top Management always finds itself in a spot to sack poor executives, as they make the best 'buddies', so they opt for the next best alternative: sack the better ones to even the statistics.

The rule of rising up in an organisation is to cling on to the branches of an upward mobile superior and grow with him but be careful not to cling onto the parasitic creeper that clings on to the same superior even while it may seemingly grow faster than the superior himself.

When you have many complaints and worries that you carry to the top management to resolve, they would be glad to give you the 'sack' to help you carry the same home.

When you live by your word you may have to leave by your boss's word.

Corollary

Stubbornness at times can lead to your being stubbed.

You are like the proverbial martini of James Bond in the organisation; you can be 'shaken, stirred' and poured out.

Persons in Top Management never get crucified alone; they always have two subordinates beside them.

Corollary

The boss may resurrect in another company but often the subordinates stay buried.

My boss like Jesus Christ said to us "Come unto me, all ye that labour and are heavy laden and I will give you rest"- and he promptly pink slipped us.

The prophecy in the Bible about "the meek will inherit the world" stands exposed in your organisation where it is: 'the company will dis-inherit the meek'.

Anyone who is says he is happy in an organisation is a trainee, and who looks happy is expecting an elevation, who says he is happy is looking to leave the organisation and who really thinks he is happy is a 'looney'.

Realise early in your career that the rules of employment are always unfair - the person who should never be up there is surprisingly always there.

People constantly switch jobs because they realise that a rolling stone gathers no boss.

You may feel that you are much better than many of your superiors but so do your subordinates.

The CEO was called the "Electric Chair" as nothing happened to him with all his failures; only the persons who came in contact with him during his failures were destroyed.

A boss who delegates a job states that he is hard pressed for time and is just following the time tested rule of delegation i.e. 'I know, I do, I do not know, I delegate'

Unreasonable milestone activities set by the boss become 'millstones' round the neck of the subordinates performing them.

Many CEO's are successful not because they are dynamic but because they are dynamite.

Seen school children performing acrobatics - where they form a pyramid with the frailest girl perched at the apex of the pyramid - so is your CEO, frail, lonely and frightened-knowing fully well that it's the shoulders of his subordinates that keeps him there.

Be wary of the accountants, when they have to make a payment they will stall it by raising a query and when they have something to deduct from you they will add even the page number and the date on your statement.

Corollary

'When Finance personnel err, the error will enhance the profits to the company and they receive accolades for their error'.

Salesmen are like snakes - when they have no venom they will hiss and frighten you and when they have venom they will rattle and frighten you - ultimately they frighten the customers away,

HRD personnel are like the chameleon -
changing colours to suit their bosses.

The PR person is one who knows all the
'inns and touts' of his trade.

In a manufacturing process, when the diameter of a wheel that is in an inaccessible area of the machinery is to be known, the Process Control man takes out a measuring tape, the Quality Control person applies an abstract formula, the engineer rings up the manufacturer and finds its diameter.

Top management stays networked with their subordinates over the 'Wine net' – the finest brewers of 'grapevine'.

If you think all persons with the same rank will be treated equally think twice - 'ranks are akin to malt, most of them become fodder for horses and a handful scotch for bosses'.

The work you carried out and which ended in failure will be named after you by your detractors but the ones you have been successful in will be forgotten even by your friends.

Corollary

Experience is learning by your failure. Rising up in the hierarchy is by yearning for your peer's failure.

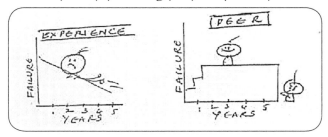

Some of your colleagues enjoy free corporate dinners and fine wine because they are the brewers of grapevine that's 'toasted' by unscrupulous bosses.

If your boss "stops the parade to pick up a penny" trample him and continue the parade.

The biggest losses of an organisation will invariably be blamed on the smallest ranked individual, probably the janitor – the chairman slipped on a wet floor that led to impaired judgment - just as many a big ship has sunk from a small leak.

The board takes all the wrong decisions but it's the lowest level employees who get sacked for implementing them.

If you are pre-determined not to hear your subordinate's explanation but just berate him - you are a blockhead who is not fit for management but sure would be great for a door frame.

Some industries lose their way but end up successful by fluke and then become the benchmark for industries that are run on sound business practices but yet do not meet success.

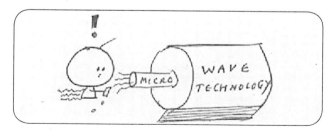

Leading from front is when you confront problems, not by being in the front of the line to leave the factory after your shift.

At times an order misunderstood and executed may yield resounding success contrary to the fact that what you had envisaged would have been an utter failure - hence always keep your orders garbled.

Remember why the the American style of Governance fails at times - They beat around the Bush, when in reality they should have beaten Bush-even before he stood for presidency. Hence, on your job 'don't beat around the bush to catch the Quail'

Remember, if the Americans had followed the principle –a Quayle in hand is worth two Bushes - they would have elected Quayle as president. While on your job, use the options available at hand to solve your problems.

Automation is defined as 'putting a pig into a machine and getting sausages out' not 'putting sausages and getting a pig out'-that's God's job.

When a boss preaches that "work is worship" in effect he means 'when you work you are worshipping me'.

Remember, Management expects you to 'Sift the data available to infer the results'-otherwise you will be s(h)ifted as a result.

A boss is a person who, when confronted for a solution to a problem, gives you a lecture on why the problem should never have arisen-since he has no solution.

Remember, there is no such thing as 'thumb rule' in reality it's only the 'dumb rule' that prevails.

Avoid learning from your experience; learn from others' failure - it's an easier alternative.

It's time to visit your astrologer when you cannot see the writing on the wall.

Corollary

Join an organisation on their terms leave on your terms.

Higher echelons of Management avoid meeting each other often as 'familiarity breeds contempt'.

It's always difficult to make minutes of a meeting in a multinational company, as the same idea expressed by persons from different countries are at times the same but sound totally different. Consider this: "the boy climbed the tree and removed the bird's nest" would be a Brit's expression, "the guy shinned up the bark and swiped the jay's bunk" would be a Yankee's expression; "He hacked the tree and whacked the nest" would be an Indian yuppie's expression- who being a computer whiz-kid uses hacking to mean 'climbing stealthily without the bird's knowledge'.

Realise these three facts early in your career

1. everybody in a given designation in the organisation will either stagnate or rise slowly unless propelled by a superior whose external force can either hasten or further retard his progress.

2. Persons who are awaiting the 'sack' will be sacked at the same speed irrespective of their level in the hierarchy of the company.

3. Whenever the possibility of your rising in the hierarchy seems bright there will also be the bright possibility of your not rising by persons working against your elevation.

Do these three 'Laws' sound familiar? they were expounded by Isaac Newton –force, acceleration, mass, time and gravity were what he unwittingly used to propound these Management laws.

Corollary

Management is the art of corroborating facts - only;
the data is manipulated to match the result.

Even when you have botched up a job
and the fault is 'glaring' feign doubt, for
all you know, your boss may never see
the fault.

Most bosses seek advice from their subordinates knowing that they will hear what they want to hear.

When there is no racial discrimination in an organisation 'similarity breeds content' or 'birds of different feathers rock together'.

If you are the boss with 'vision' make
sure that this 'vision' does not turn out
to be your subordinate's 'nightmare'.

When you can commit a mistake that
you will condemn in others and yet get
away –you must be the CEO.

Always leave the company on Medical grounds your 'payments' due in all probability will not be inordinately delayed - unless you were so bad that the Management preferred you dead.

When you attend official parties make sure that you maintain a 'spirit level' that ensures that the floor is not vertical.

Corollary

When you think that you are climbing steps holding the handrails - you may be in fact drunk and crawling on the railway track.

Believe in 'spirits' they are a benevolent solvent to dissolve complex problems — they 'cheer' you up and reduce the 'fear' of failures.

Even when you feel you are good at your work, you must work with the fear that you must be the change that the organisation wants to see.

Like Mark Anthony you must be wondering why your many good achievents are invariably forgotten and the only bad one is highlighted always by your bosses. That is because your bosses are always Brutus.

Remember that 'Logic' is only used when you do not have the right answer-it can prove any solution being contemplated as either right or wrong depending on how strongly you oppose or support the person giving the solution.

When your qualification exceeds your intelligence – you are fit for top management only.

Remember maintenance is a skilled job – as inferred from the Quote - "that's what the mechanic thought when his wife sought maintenance on divorce and he informed the judge that she was too dumb for maintenance but maybe administration would suit her better".

Many have seen apples fall from trees but only Newton attributed 'gravity' to the fall - others saw the apple for lunch. Similarly, many can see the problem but only one sees the solution.

remember wealth is rarely earned it's either inherited or ordained by destiny - it's only when you have it that you realise that you have to make it look as a planned success and write your speeches and memoirs accordingly.

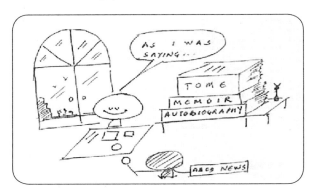

Remember if it's anyone you have to fear-it's always your peer.

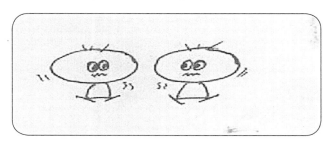

Remember that anger is always vented on a person who has nothing to do with the cause - invariably on the meekest.

Remember it's what's spoken about you amongst your colleagues that define your character.

Remember he who runs away from problems keeps changing jobs till he ends up being consultant-offering solutions to the same problems he ran away from.

Remember at times it pays to be an astrologer to your boss - predict that his elevation or exit will happen three days after yours.

Remember your qualification teaches you how a thing should work but its knowledge that teaches you why it failed to work.

Before you offer a solution, remember that successful original ideas are never attributed to the originator while failed ideas will be named after the originator.

Don't be carried away by the advice 'failure is the stepping stone to success'- in reality you become the stepping stone for others' success.

Remember that a bank will always lend money to an entrepreneur for starting a business but will never give him working capital to run it and repay his loan.

It's only the boss who can be happy without reason and angry without cause.

Remember in a corporate the director's salary has no ceiling while yours is anchored to the floor.

Remember that a job done by consensus is done by one who knows not his job.

Corollary

A decision by consensus is invariably 'nonsensus'

When your colleague beats you to the goal - its time you left via the goal posts.

Remember super session is the art of creating no succession.

When you are outdone by your colleague for an elevation - the grapes need not necessarily be sour, they will be bitter.

If your subordinate waves a sword to chase a fly buzzing around you nose- that's sycophancy, however if your nose gets cut by a swishing sword then it's your boss.

Always beware of flatterers they will invariably leave you when you are flattened.

A donkey never wags its tail when it sees its master - be careful when an idiotic subordinate seems very friendly.

Always 'cry wolf' on the first two occasions in your job, you will have help on hand, and then find another job.

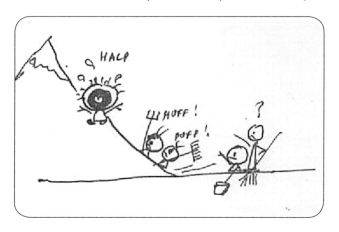

Remember the story of the honest woodcutter who was rewarded with three axes - you may not want even one in your job even when you are very honest person.

Remember a sycophant is just a pedestal that supports the boots of his superior.

Remember failure is attributed to a person while success is attributed to the organisation.

Remember that you may fall of a cliff and yet land safely on moss and avoid injury, however, in your job if you fall it will invariably be outside the gates of your organisation.

Management personnel are akin to a famous quote on the American presidency – "George Washington never lied, Nixon never told the truth and Reagan never knew the difference".

Remember that only in your imagination can you rise by leaps and bounds in the hierarchy without the actual experience.

Corollary

There is no gain in expertise when there is no pain in work

You have the right to remain incompetent till you are 'pink slipped'.

Truth never need be rehearsed – while lies are a complex algorithm that ultimately lead to the truth, that you are lying.

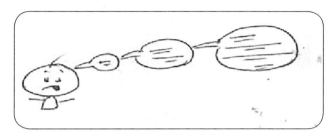

It is not the number of years of experience but the number of years of learning that advances your career-"experience is a fossil while learning is living".

There are two types of executives in every organisation - one brings about change and the other is about to be changed.

The leader is the one who is permitted to think and the others believe in his thinking - till the battle is lost.

All organisations run on the philosophy of Socrates - "success comes to a group of donkeys led by a lion over a group of lions led by a donkey".

An expert committee is a group were everyone talks of possible solutions but never reaches a consensus on one - this is left to another expert committee.

'An expert invariably is never a leader but only a dealer who holds all the aces'.

When, an engineer makes a mistake, he can lose his job; when, an accountant makes a mistake, he can lose his job; when, an HR manager makes a mistake, he can lose his job, when, the CEO makes a mistake, the engineer, accountant and the HR manager can lose their jobs.

Remember you will surely be replaced once you teach your subordinate your job.

A trainer teaches you the job while a mentor preaches you the job.

Remember 'Bragging is like looking at the sun through a magnifying glass'.

Just like still waters run deep - when in a deep problem keep still.

Remember, the saying 'Across the Nile in a tub, he came and drowned in a manhole'-it's the small problems that invariably land you in major trouble.

Remember, work is worship(ing) your boss.

The pearl is an irritant to the oyster -
When you are an irritant to your boss
you may be the pearl to his boss.

There are always two types of Managers,
one 'walks the talk' and the other 'talks
and walks away"

Given some work–'your attitude begins to implement while your ego fishes for compliments'.

Most Managers are "I told you" types, who tell you to act with caution at the start of an assignment even while not knowing an iota of how to do the assignment.

In most organisations, the 'survival of the (mis) fittest' is the rule - not the exception. However it is the (miss) fittest who gets the job of the steno.

The theory of effective management started when "the ape held up his spine and became a man"; choose what you want to be in your organisation: an ape or a man with a spine.

Corollary

Remember it's only in the Bible you can produce a woman from a rib, in your organisation it requires an 'entire spine to produce a man'.

Remember "you may have all the power and wealth, but you will get your food only because the farmer decides to grow it". It is the same in your organisation, it's your subordinates who give you the aura of success.

Remember you will only love your job when people around you know your job.

Remember your ends will never meet, as your boss is the other end.

Never think of leisure if you are a hard worker, as hard work begets more hard work.

If you are good, your subordinates will propel you up, your peers repel you and your bosses compel you to stay.

Be like a tortoise in your work - use your subordinates and peers as your legs and shell to move you forward and only stick out your neck at the finishing line.

Remember history always talks of leaders, never of their subordinates.

Remember George Bush's description of himself in a blooper as a 'Master of Low Expectation' this fits the description of an employee in your organisation who will be the 'MOLE' working for your competitor while maintaining a low profile in your organisation.

Any edeavour to succeed requires Knowledge, Effort and Resources - it's invariably achieved by a team and then the success will be attributed to the one who gave the resources and the ones who provided the knowledge and effort join in the group photo.

Listing in as many faults-both real and imaginary - that can arise before the start of any new endeavour is the 'insurance' the boss takes to protect his image in the event the endeavour fails.

Remember in teamwork when ideas are divided (everyone is thinking) actions after deliberations are united and when ideas are united (only one is thinking- the boss) actions after deliberations are divided.

The boss was impressing upon his subordinates the importance of learning their job-'Give a man a fish and you give him a meal, teach him to fish and you give him a life,' he said - the next day all his subordinates were out fishing.

Communication is an art that one must master-never make your boss happy by telling him after a frustrating day at work that you would like to retire, when you meant just go and sleep.

No boss is nice to a subordinate who he perceives is better than him-he will use all his efforts and resources to blunt the 'better', hence if you are a subordinate always carry the benign smile of stupidity before your boss.

Merit is the most subjective word in management - you can spend your entire career being stupid and yet seem meritorious.

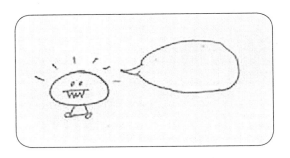

In War: you may lose the battle but yet win the war.

In De-addiction: you have to lose the bar to win over the bottle.

CEO at work: you have to raise the bar, bottle feed your subordinates, win the battle of the board room —and yet you may lose the war and your job.

Remember that a hero is good in deeds, a zero in words—as he would have talked himself out of the deeds.

MANAGEMENT SYLLABUS TAUGHT AT PRIMARY SCHOOL

The Black sheep has three bags of wool while the white one has more meat.

Corollary

At work he who betrays makes more money, the honest is 'eaten'.

When you climb uphill you will fall with
your pail just as Jack did.

Corollary

At work 'uphill' tasks will cause your 'downhill'
ride.

When you want to feed the dog look in
the cupboard for a bone as old Mother
Hubbard did.

Corollary

Imagine what would have happened if Mother
Hubbard saw a skeleton in the cupboard while
searching for a bone. Would she have fed the dog?

Corollary

Never reveal the skeleton in your cupboard even if it means starving the dog.

In Twinkle Twinkle little star, the bright star is always 'up above the world so high', when you are bright you may shine far outside the organisation gates, the dull invariably are inside.

Jack Spratt and his wife licked their plate clean even when they had diametrically opposite eating habits - When you don't work as a team you will be 'licked'.

Remember Mary had a Little Lamb - the lamb was a source of joy to the other children in school - when you are as meek as a lamb you will also be a source of joy to your peers and superiors - when cooked.

Remember, the cat fiddled and the cow jumped over the moon and the dish ran away with the spoon-If you keep fiddling, somebody will overtake you and you will lose all your belongings.

The clock struck one and the mouse ran down.

Corollary

What did the clock strike? - One O' clock or one mouse?

Corollary

When the Management strikes one, make sure you are not the one.

Try not to be a 'Humpty - Dumpty'- if someone has to fall, try coaxing your colleague.

The fundamental law of your job - rock -a-bye baby, when the wind blows the cradle will rock, when the bough breaks, the cradle will fall, down will come baby, cradle and all.

In the event you make a mistake, be like little Bo-Peep - who lost her sheep and left them alone and they came home by themselves - the mistake at times resolves itself.

Remember-Row-row-row your boat gently down the streamz, merrily, merrily, merrily, life is such a dream - similarly gently steer you path amongst your colleagues and you will reach your goals merrily.

Remember an organisation is like Old Mac Donald's farm - he had ducks like you EIEIO, and a pig CE(IEI)O.

Success will come to you if you work like little Jack Horner - who sat in a corner, eating his christmas pie, put in his thumb pulled out a plum and said "what a good boy am I"-do your job and praise yourself and you will be happy, expect your boss to praise you and he will want your pie.

Remember Aesop's tale of the thirsty Pigeon that ran into a billboard containing a picture of a goblet of water and fell down with broken wings - similarly at work in pursuit of success you should not fall into an open manhole.

INDEX OF LIFE

In life you can be a Hero or a Nero - either make others play second fiddle or you fiddle alone.

Rate the factors that govern your life like, Health, Wealth, Character, Happiness and Honesty, on a scale of 0 to 10 and you will be surprised to find that the product is a constant for all humans - As Honesty is the leveler.

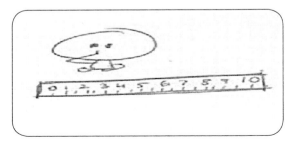

Many brilliant youngsters just out of college are like seeds when they join an organisation, some get pecked by birds and perish, some bloom to beautiful flowers for a brief period and a few who become CEO's are like cacti, prickly and blooming occasionally.

Decision making in most businesses is akin to the tyres of an automobile with ethics being one of the front tyres and the other three being profit. Invariably it's only ethics that has a flat and is replaced by the stepney which is also profit.

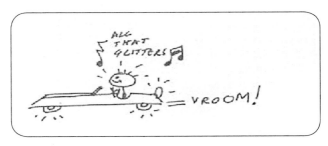

The term 'ethical business' is an oxymoron that only morons visualise.

When you are more qualified than your intelligence you will have an inferiority complex.

Your length of service is an experiment it's the depth of your knowledge that is experience.

The proof of your working lies in what's eating your boss.

The proof of you having worked is based on what your boss sees as what's left of his work.

You cannot sleep over your work and expect your boss to dream the job's done.

You will never be remembered for what you did but for what you got done —even if done cruelly - no one credits the building of the Taj Mahal to the thousands of artisans who had their hands chopped off after building it, but Emperor Shah Jahan in spite of his cruelty is credited for this magnificent monument of love.

Sweat does not at all the time mean success —most of the time it implies fear.

Only persons within the family tree of the proprietor rise for free in an organisation. others go underground to become the roots that hold the family tree. That is why the 'son never sets outside the boardroom'

Ingenuity is in changing the graduation in the scale to increase turnover.

The magnitude of your cruelty is directly proportional to your weakness.

Success is always team effort while failure is your birthright-never give it up.

When refining silver, gold is a contaminant - in many an organisation, when mediocrity is the rule, merit can become a liability.

Remember your failures are the stepping stones that your peers use to pave their progress.

Anger and stress are not the by product of your work; it is the bye product of your frustration - your rise in salary is never directly proportional to the rise in your blood pressure and blood sugar readings.

Skilled employees rarely rise, as they are kept anchored to their areas of expertise; it is the unskilled like flotsam that drift into the boardrooms.

Like hunger makes an ordinary meal tasty, anger mars your appreciation of the good in your subordinates.

If you have been in your organisation long, you will realise that it's like a marathon - 'time will wound your heels'.

A 'tit for tat' attitude will make the world 'titless'.

Corollary

Why lose a tit for a tat that no one knows what it is.

When you are constantly being rotated to various departments with the refrain you are being trained it's an indication that your virtues and abilities are not in demand.

When you are overjoyed with the elevation you just got in your job, in all probability you did not deserve it – to the deserving, promotion is matter of routine.

To reach the summit is an arduous task but to fall off of it is easy.

When there are ten persons in your group and nine join together, they become a formidable group but the single one becomes their leader-more formidable.

Corollary

United, you are a union, divided, you can be their leader.

'A good idea will always be overtaken, opposed and defeated by a bad idea coming from the same direction' is the 'third law of ideas' in the organisation.

Corollary

A good idea weighed by solid facts will always sink and only bad ideas supported on hollow reasoning will float.

A management that lacks authority always resorts to overstaffing.

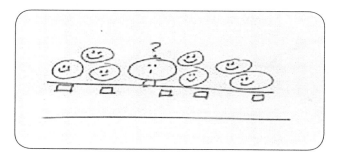

A good boss is one who knows to discriminate between you and the rest.

Those who lose learn, those who win earn.

Experience starts with a shut mouth and an open mind.

Never create the divide and then try to bridge it.

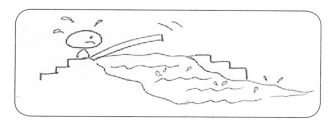

Small problems require intelligent solutions, big ones bold solutions.

PROFILE OF THE AUTHOR

Balasubramaniam is a qualified Engineer having worked for more than three decades in Industry and Engineering consultancy. With his passion for writing, he decided to temporarily switch tracks by entering the field of penmanship. His expertise and interests in the field of Technology, Management and Sociology, have led him to write on these subjects.

He has considerable experience in working with a wide cross section of engineers, scientists and administrators having niche expertise in various areas of Engineering and Management. Combining his sense of humour with a storehouse of knowledge on behavioral science by observing persons taking decisions under various circumstances he has transformed this knowledge to 'quips' that provide a comic interlude in the sublime understanding of the art of Management to the discerning reader.

He is a motivational speaker and writer who gives talks to students on current subjects relating to Technology, Sociology and Management with intent to advance knowledge to them.

His first book on Sociology was on the Badaga community of The Nilgiris, Tamilnadu This book was titled: Paamé - The History and culture of the Badagas of the Nilgiris. The book was well received by readers of Sociology, Anthropology and History.

Living in the Nilgiris, he endears himself to the hills by his long walks amidst nature's trails. He claims that these walks permit him to live in the silent companionship of his thoughts that provide him the elixir for his writings.